Contents

Bon Voyage!

How to Use This Travel Guide

Before we embark on our first Internet field trip, here are a few travel tips you'll want to know:

The Tour Guide and the Traveler

In this book, you, the teacher, are the "tour guide." It might feel like a demotion, but we prefer to think of it as a step up. Throughout these trips the "travelers" (or students) are invited to create their own learning experiences. The activity pages and directions act as a starting point. As the tour guide, your job is not to dole out knowledge but to invite the travelers to learn for themselves. In this position you become the helpful "guide on the side" rather than "sage on the stage."

The Starting Point

All the journeys in this book depart from one online "depot" or Web site:

www.scholastic.com/profbooks/easyinternet/10fieldtrips.htm

Remember to bookmark this site or add it to your favorites. All the Web sites your travelers will need to complete the activities in this book can be found under this single URL. To reach a virtual destination, just click on the hot links under the name of the activity you're working on.

10 QUICK & FUN
INTERNET
FIELD TRIPS

Instant Activity Sheets That Guide Kids on Internet Learning Journeys—From Ellis Island to Mars— and Enhance the Topics You Teach!

by Deirdre Kelly

SCHOLASTIC
PROFESSIONAL BOOKS

New York • Toronto • London • Auckland • Sydney
Mexico City • New Delhi • Hong Kong • Buenos Aires

- -

Dedication

Dedicated to Hilary, because our children
take us on the best journeys of our lives.

Love,
Mommy

- -

Cover design by **Norma Ortiz**
Interior design by **Holly Grundon**
Interior illustrations by **Drew Hires**

ISBN 0-439-27165-7
Copyright © 2001 by Deirdre Kelly
Printed in the U.S.A.

As with any online activity, you'll want to make sure that you are comfortable with the Web sites before taking your students to them. Web-site content is subject to change without notice, so make sure you're familiar with the sites in this or any other Web-activity book. (We will be checking the links regularly to ensure that the sites we suggest are still working and continue to offer the content materials your travelers need to complete the activity.) Ultimately, it is your responsibility to provide educational, safe, and interesting resources for your students.

You might want to review Internet safety rules with students before sending them on their way. Photocopy and laminate the "Travel Tips" on page 7 and post it next to each computer.

Skill Levels

Each of our trips promotes different skills—some require higher-level thinking than others. Since this book is designed for 3rd through 6th grades, we needed to offer a variety of levels. Feel free to modify the assignments to increase or decrease the challenge level to fit the needs of your travelers.

The Accidental Tourist

The "accidents" or unintended lessons of learning are sometimes the best experiences students can have. If an activity designed to do one thing turns into something else entirely, just run with it. You'll notice that there is no answer key in the back of this book—that's intentional. These activities are designed to be open-ended, allowing students to construct their own knowledge. There also isn't a great deal of background information or teacher direction for each activity. You can find the background information for each topic within the Web sites. You will definitely want to study the sites before taking your travelers there. Student directions on each activity page have been designed so that you can construct the activity from them. Different teachers are likely to interpret and deliver these activities in different ways, and that's just fine with us!

Excursions Off the Beaten Path

Just like a real trip, flexibility is key. If your students see an interesting side trip off one of the main trips, by all means take it. If you want to stay at a destination longer than the "tour" allows, then stop and take the time you need to fully appreciate the area.

Virtual Permission Slip

Use the humorous permission slip on page 8 to generate some interest in your Internet field trip, as well as get permission for your students to participate in online activities. Fill in the destination blank with locations such as Ancient Greece and Mars and see how fast these permission slips come back to your in box!

Travel Tips

These are your rules of the road for online travels in our classroom. Remember, don't leave home(page) without them!

Hey! Where Am I?

Pay attention to where your cyberpath is taking you! Your tour guide (teacher) gave you someplace to go—make sure you get there. You should always stay where your teacher asked you to be.

What Time Is It?

You shouldn't find yourself wandering around aimlessly. You've got a job to do—make sure you're doing it! Here's a helpful trick: When you sit down in front of the computer to start your activity, record the time in the upper left-hand corner of your paper. This way, you'll be able to tell how long you've been online.

Empty Hands?

If you've walked over to the computer to use the Internet and you have nothing in your hands, that's the first sign of a problem. You're supposed to be using the Internet in order to do something specific, such as find information or figure something out. You should at least have paper and pencil with you.

When in Doubt, Go Home!

If you've bumped into something inappropriate or unexpected, use the "Home" button on your Web browser to take you back to your homepage. Then let your teacher know what happened.

Virtual Permission Slip

Dear Parents:

You'll be happy to know that I'm taking the class on a field trip to _____!
Our trip is scheduled for _____/_____/_____. I'm sure it will be a great trip, full of new learning experiences and many new memories.

In order to attend this virtual trip, your child will need to return this permission slip with your signature.

Thanks so much for your support. We'll see you when we get back!

Signed,

_____
(Tour Guide)

Yes, I give permission for my child _____
                                                    (name)

to attend this (virtual) field trip to _____.
                                                    (destination)

_____
(Parent signature)

Grand Canyon

It's Not Just a Hole, It's an Adventure!

Travel Plan

Pack your bags and hop on board! We're off to the Grand Canyon! There's much to see and do at this world-famous hole in the ground, so let's get busy. On this trip, travelers will collect important information about the Grand Canyon, plan a trip to the canyon, and finally travel back in time with explorer John Wesley Powell!

Trip Planner

Trip Title: Canyon Calculations
Objective: Travelers will collect and record data from an online source.
Skills: Estimation, data collection

Trip Title: Grand Plans
Objective: Travelers will manage a fictional budget and utilize online data in a decision-making process.
Skills: Organization, decision making

Trip Title: The Adventures of J.W. Powell
Objective: Travelers will gather and prioritize data from an online source.
Skills: Making judgments, decision making

Itinerary

Steer students to this online "depot" to start their virtual journey on the Web. Just click on the hot links below the activity title to "transport" students to the Web sites they need to complete the activity.

www.scholastic.com/profbooks/easyinternet/10fieldtrips.htm

Name: _____   Date: _____

Canyon Calculations

www.scholastic.com/profbooks/easyinternet/10fieldtrips.htm

Directions Click on the links under this Web site to answer the questions on this travel page. Remember: The trick to collecting information is to get a lay of the land first (check things out, look around, see what's there to see), and then start answering questions!

---

1 **How big is the Grand Canyon?**

Length: _____

Depth: _____

Width: _____

2 **According to the Web site, how long would it take to walk to the bottom of the Grand Canyon and back out?** _____

3 **Since you know how long it would take you to walk the canyon, you can probably figure out other methods of transportation, too. How long do you think it would take you to travel into the Grand Canyon using one of these methods?**

Rollerblade: _____   Hangglider: _____

4-wheel-drive jeep: _____   Run: _____

4 **Speaking of travel, how many miles did YOU have to travel to get to Grand Canyon from your city?**

From _____ to Grand Canyon,
          (your city and state)

Arizona, is _____ miles.

How'd you figure that out? _____

Show your travel thinking! _____

_____

5 **How old do you think is the Grand Canyon?** _____

How'd you figure that out? _____

_____

Grand Plans

www.scholastic.com/profbooks/easyinternet/10fieldtrips.htm

Directions Plan a five-day trip to the Grand Canyon using only the information you find on this Web site. You have $1,000 to spend. How you spend the money is up to you! Good luck, campers!

1 **When will you go? Month:** _____ **Dates:** _____

  Why have you chosen that time? _____

2 **Where will you stay?** _____

  Why did you choose this location? _____

  Cost: _____

3 **How will you travel around the Grand Canyon?**

  Transportation: _____ **Cost:** _____

4 **Where will you eat? How much will you spend on food?**

  Daily food allowance: _____ **Cost:** _____

  Eating establishments: _____

5 **What kinds of activities will you do while you're there?**

  Activities: _____

  _____

  Locations: _____

  _____

  Cost: _____

6 **What will you pack to take with you? Don't just take clothes. You'll need to take a few other things, depending on when you'll be traveling. Make a list on the back of this paper. Be sure you can explain WHY you'll be taking these particular items.**

The Adventures of J. W. Powell

www.scholastic.com/profbooks/easyinternet/10fieldtrips.htm

Directions Click on the links under this Web site to retrace the steps of John Wesley Powell and his expedition down the Colorado River. Read Powell's travel logs and decide which four events from the expedition are the most important—and why. Fill in the organizer below. Then find out which events received the most votes from the rest of the class.

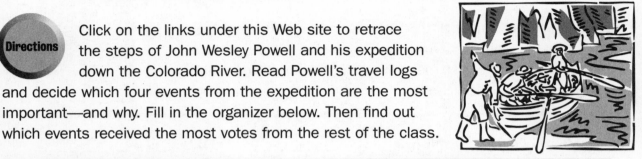

Event: _____

Briefly describe what happened:

Why is this event one of your top 4?

Event: _____

Briefly describe what happened:

Why is this event one of your top 4?

Event: _____

Briefly describe what happened:

Why is this event one of your top 4?

Event: _____

Briefly describe what happened:

Why is this event one of your top 4?

Washington, D.C.

Our Nation's Capital

Travel Plan

Washington, D.C., is one of the most impressive cities in the world. This beautiful city is rich in culture and history. During this trip, travelers will get to know our nation's capital by visiting its major landmarks.

Trip Planner

Trip Title: Welcome Home!

Objective: Travelers will complete a KWL chart based on the White House.

Skill: Information management

Trip Title: Let's Go to the Mall!

Objective: Travelers will use detailed information about the history and monuments of the National Mall to create a model of the Mall.

Skill: Deductive reasoning

Trip Title: Monumental Messages

Objective: Travelers will speculate on what our national monuments tell the rest of the world about the American people.

Skill: Recognition of relationships and patterns

Itinerary

Steer students to this online "depot" to start their virtual journey on the Web. Just click on the hot links below the activity title to "transport" students to the Web sites they need to complete the activity.

www.scholastic.com/profbooks/easyinternet/10fieldtrips.htm

Name: _____ **Date:** _____

Welcome Home!

www.scholastic.com/profbooks/easyinternet/10fieldtrips.htm

 Click on the links under this Web site to visit the White House. Before you go, fill in the KWL chart below. Write everything you KNOW about the White House in the first column and what you WANT TO KNOW in the second column. Brainstorm as many questions as possible. When you're finished, go to the site and search for proof of what you know and for answers to your questions. Take notes of what you've LEARNED in the third column. Use the back of this page if you need more space.

K	W	L

Name: _____ **Date:** _____

Let's Go to the Mall!

www.scholastic.com/profbooks/easyinternet/10fieldtrips.htm

Directions Click on the links below this Web site to tour the National Mall and other famous D.C. sites. Take careful notes below about the monuments and buildings that make up the Mall and their locations. Then construct a model or map of the National Mall and the city based on your notes.

Mall Location	Clues About Location/Positioning	Web Site Reference
Washington Monument & Capitol Building	"...view of the Mall looking from the Washington Monument to the Capitol building — they're lined up with one another"	Camera Over Washington

> **Compare your finished map or model with the map of Washington, D.C., on the Web to see how well you read the clues!**

Name: _____ **Date:** _____

Monumental Messages

www.scholastic.com/profbooks/easyinternet/10fieldtrips.htm

Directions Click on the links below this Web site to explore the monuments in our nation's capital. Pay close attention to the subject or subjects honored by each monument. What do our monuments tell the world about the American people and the ideals that we value?

Monument	Subject	Ideals We Value
Washington Monument	George Washington, the first president	Leadership, personal courage, liberty, democracy

Canada & Mexico

Our Neighbors

Travel Plan

Get ready for some challenges as travelers venture from the tropics to the tundra on this trip. Make sure students bring along plenty of thinking skills, and they'll be just fine!

Trip Planner

Trip Title: Our Neighbors to the North and South

Objective: Travelers will use a graphic organizer to collect and organize information.

Skill: Data collection

Trip Title: Venn Again, Maybe We're Not So Different!

Objective: Travelers will collect data to create a Venn diagram and identify differences and similarities among three countries.

Skill: Synthesis of data

Trip Title: We Were Here First!

Objective: Travelers will collect and organize information on ancient cultures.

Skill: Data collection (without research topics)

Itinerary

Steer students to this online "depot" to start their virtual journey on the Web. Just click on the hot links below the activity title to "transport" students to the Web sites they need to complete the activity.

www.scholastic.com/profbooks/easyinternet/10fieldtrips.htm

Name: _____   Date: _____

Our Neighbors to the North and South

www.scholastic.com/profbooks/easyinternet/10fieldtrips.htm

 Directions Click on the links under this Web site to complete the chart below. Compare the geography, government, and people of these two fascinating countries. Then pick another area you'd like to compare (e.g., language, food).

Topics	Mexico	Canada
Geography		
Government		
People		
What else? _____		

Name: _____ **Date:** _____

Venn Again, Maybe We're Not So Different!

www.scholastic.com/profbooks/easyinternet/10fieldtrips.htm

Directions
After your virtual visit to the sun-soaked beaches of Mexico and the wilds of Canada (page 18), complete the Venn diagram below to compare these countries with the U.S.A. Record information specific to the individual countries in the circles. Identify similarities in the overlapping areas.

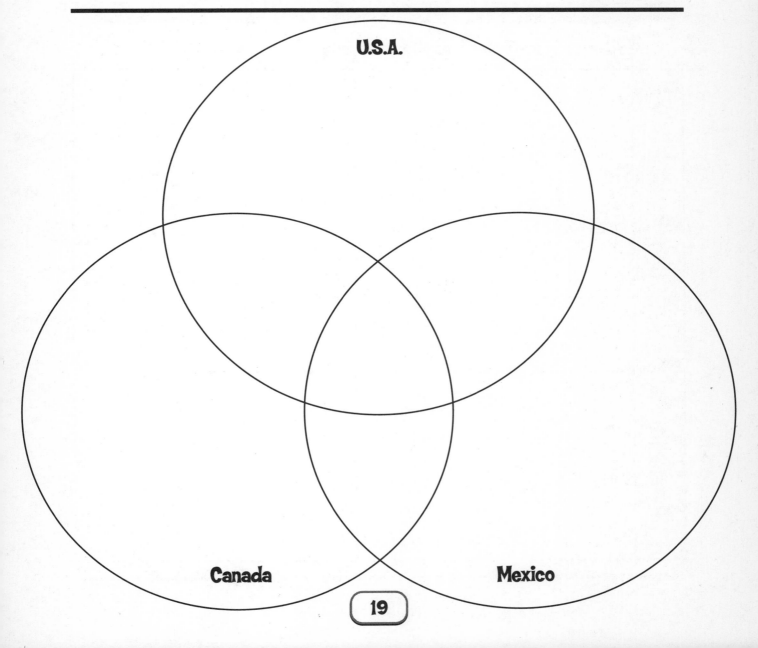

U.S.A.

Canada   Mexico

We Were Here First!

www.scholastic.com/profbooks/easyinternet/10fieldtrips.htm

Directions Click on the links under this Web site to gather information about the ancient cultures of Mexico and Canada. Record as much information as you can in the area below. Then develop a descriptive sentence about these ancient cultures. Use your best research skills to figure out the names of these cultures.

	Canada's Ancient Cultures	Mexico's Ancient Cultures
Information		
Description		

The Rain Forest

Travel Plan

Pack up your tropical-weather gear, ropes, cameras, and some bug spray. We're off to the rain forest! Travelers will trek through these tropical jungles, check out the animals, and look for ways to help save the rain forest.

Trip Planner

Trip Title: And So It Goes…
Objective: Travelers will read and summarize nonfiction information.
Skills: Summarization, information management

Trip Title: Rain Forest Olympics
Objective: Travelers will recognize and compare specialized adaptations of rain-forest creatures.
Skill: Synthesis

Trip Title: Stamping Out Destruction
Objective: Travelers will evaluate and choose from a collection of ecologically responsible actions.
Skill: Evaluation

Itinerary

Steer students to this online "depot" to start their virtual journey on the Web. Just click on the hot links below the activity title to "transport" students to the Web sites they need to complete the activity.

www.scholastic.com/profbooks/easyinternet/10fieldtrips.htm

And So It Goes...

www.scholastic.com/profbooks/easyinternet/10fieldtrips.htm

Directions As a top investigative reporter for a newsmagazine show, you've been chosen to travel to and report on Earth's tropical forests. Remember that a good investigative reporter finds the answers to all the important questions: Who, What, When, Where, Why, and How. "What" is the destruction of the planet's rain forests. Click on the links under this Web site to help you find answers to the other questions.

WHO? (Who is doing it? Who is affected by it?)

HOW? (How can it be stopped? How can it be fixed?)

What? Destruction of the Planet's Rain Forests

WHEN? (How long has it been going on? When must it be stopped?)

WHERE? (Where is this happening?)

WHY? (Why is this happening? Why should we care?)

You have four minutes of on-air time to tell the complete story about rain forests. Use the back of this page to write your "copy" for the teleprompter. Practice a few times to make sure your report lasts exactly four minutes.

Name: _____   **Date:** _____

Rain Forest Olympics

www.scholastic.com/profbooks/easyinternet/10fieldtrips.htm

Directions You have been appointed leader of the Rain Forest Olympics Committee to help raise money to preserve the rain forests. Your job is to design an Olympic games for the creatures of the rain forest. Click on the links under this Web site to study the animals, observe their natural abilities, and take note of their special talents (e.g., tree swinging, root climbing). Record your findings below.

Animal	Special Talents/Abilities

**Use the back of this page to create the events that
will become part of the first Rain Forest Olympics!**
HINT: Think about the real Olympic events to get ideas (like the 200-yard canopy crawl).

Name: _____   **Date:** _____

Stamping Out Destruction

www.scholastic.com/profbooks/easyinternet/10fieldtrips.htm

Directions Create a stamp that the post office could sell to raise money to save rain forests across the globe! Click on the links under this Web site for references. Then take out your sketch pad (or use the space below) and begin drawing.

The South Pole

The Bottom of the Earth

Travel Plan

Grab your cold-weather gear and board
a ship to the South Pole! On this trip,
travelers will examine the changing
shape of Antarctica and determine the
ownership of this winter wonderland.

Trip Planner

Trip Title: Packing Is Such Sweet Sorrow
Objective: Travelers will use critical-thinking and logical-reasoning skills
to decide what to pack on a trip to Antarctica.
Skill: Comprehension

Trip Title: Breaking Up Is Hard to Do
Objective: Travelers will create a cause-and-effect graphic organizer.
Skill: Cause-and-effect relationships

Trip Title: Whose Snow Is This?
Objective: Travelers will explore the idea of territorial claims.
Skill: Evaluation

Itinerary

Steer students to this online "depot" to start their virtual journey on
the Web. Just click on the hot links below the activity title to "transport"
students to the Web sites they need to complete the activity.

www.scholastic.com/profbooks/easyinternet/10fieldtrips.htm

Name: _____   **Date:** _____

Packing Is Such Sweet Sorrow

www.scholastic.com/profbooks/easyinternet/10fieldtrips.htm

Directions   You're off to the frozen continent! Brainstorm a list of items you'll take with you and record it under "Stuff to Pack." Number the items, using 1 for the most important item to bring. Then click on the links under this Web site to check the packing list of an actual expedition to Antarctica. Did you forget anything important? Write those items in the "Don't Forget!" section. Did you bring anything that was not on the packing list? Put those items under "Leave Behind." Discuss your lists as a class. What items are really important and why?

Stuff to Pack

Don't Forget!

Leave Behind

Name: _____   **Date:** _____

Breaking Up Is Hard to Do

www.scholastic.com/profbooks/easyinternet/10fieldtrips.htm

Directions An iceberg the size of Connecticut has broken off the coastline of Antarctica! Your boss will want answers to two questions: "What caused this to happen?" and "What will happen as a result of this?" Click on the links under this Web site to learn more about icebergs and their effects. Then jot your notes in the boxes below, based on your knowledge of Antarctica's environment and ecology.

Causes   Effects

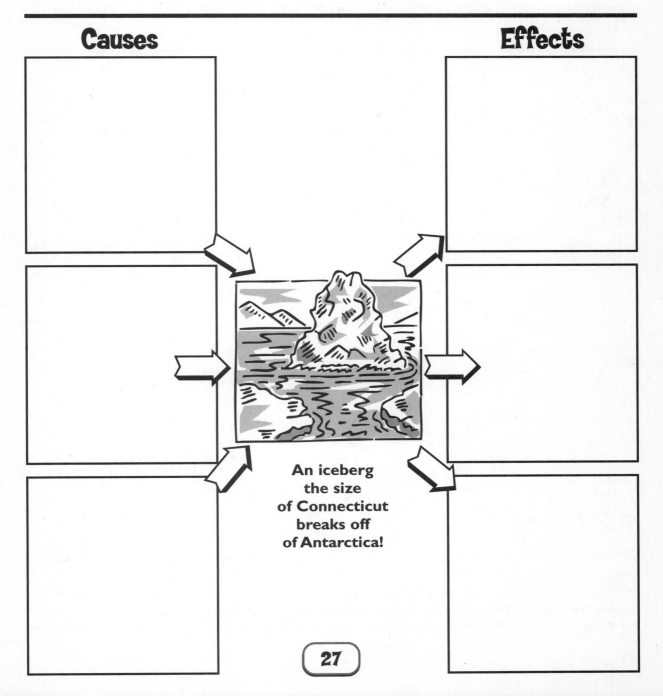

An iceberg the size of Connecticut breaks off of Antarctica!

Name: _____   Date: _____

Whose Snow Is This?

www.scholastic.com/profbooks/easyinternet/10fieldtrips.htm

Directions You're in a meeting with several other countries, each hoping to claim a piece of Antarctica to be part of its own country. Use the map below to show what portion of the land you want. Then convince the others why you deserve this section and come to an agreement. Remember that not all the land is equally valuable. For example, would a landlocked section serve your purposes? Develop some ground rules or treaty with the different countries about sharing the land.

Team Name: _____   **Country Name:** _____

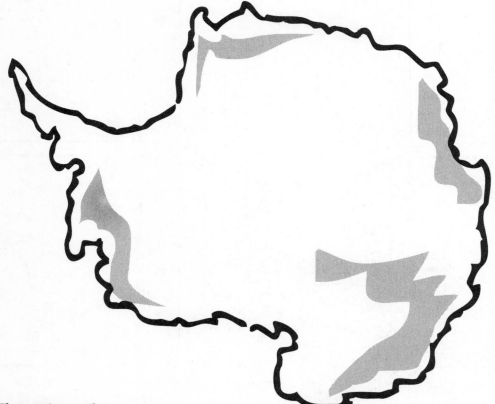

The Treaty

On the back of this paper, brainstorm a few rules that you'd like to put in the treaty. Once all the teams are ready, get together with your lists and create a treaty for Antarctica. After you've created your virtual treaty, click on the link under the above Web site to compare your treaty to the real one!

Mars

The Red Planet

Travel Plan

This trip might take a while. After all, Mars is almost 50 million miles away from Earth! To pass the time, challenge travelers to learn as much as they can about the Red Planet. Ready? Almost time for liftoff! 10—9—8—7…

Trip Planner

Trip Title: Martian Math
Objective: Travelers will create and solve a variety of Mars-themed word problems.
Skill: Information management

Trip Title: Future Study: Mars
Objective: Travelers will extrapolate events into the future based on the fictional colonization of Mars.
Skills: Synthesis, group dynamics, creativity

Trip Title: Eek! A Martian!
Objective: Travelers will create alien beings that have adapted to the Martian environment.
Skills: Synthesis, creativity

Itinerary

Steer students to this online "depot" to start their virtual journey on the Web. Just click on the hot links below the activity title to "transport" students to the Web sites they need to complete the activity.

www.scholastic.com/profbooks/easyinternet/10fieldtrips.htm

Name: _____   **Date:** _____

Martian Math

www.scholastic.com/profbooks/easyinternet/10fieldtrips.htm

Directions Bet you never thought a visit to Mars can be a math-filled adventure! Landing on the planet itself brings to mind several math problems—from your craft's rate of descent to the number of bounces it makes before coming to a complete stop. Click on the links under this Web site to study the Red Planet, then write your Mars-related math problems below. Swap with a friend and solve some Martian math!

The Trip to Mars

The Landing

Exploring the Surface

Conducting Experiments

Liftoff From Mars

The Trip Back Home

Name: _____   Date: _____

Future Study: Mars

www.scholastic.com/profbooks/easyinternet/10fieldtrips.htm

Directions The Mars Colonization Project has just been completed, and Mars is ready for colonists to live on its surface. But sending Earthlings to this far-off place raises many concerns. Click on the links under this Web site to learn more about colonizing Mars. Then think about the questions below and answer them.

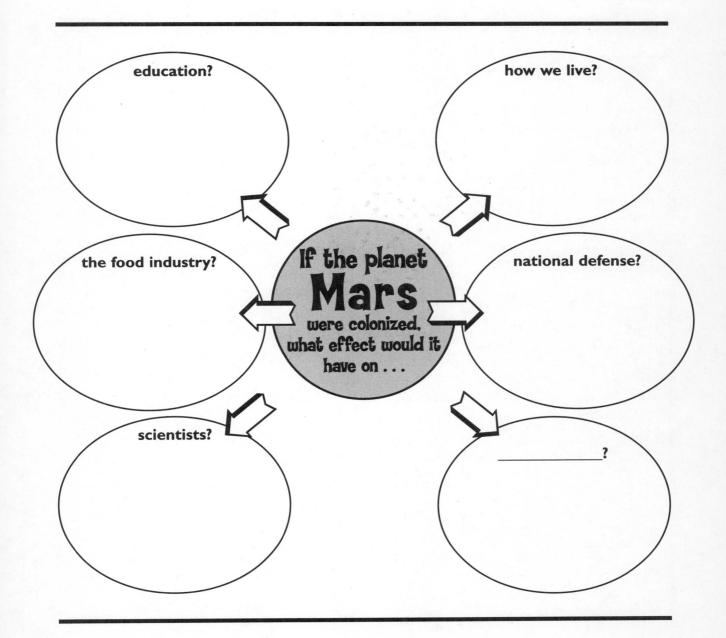

education?

how we live?

the food industry?

If the planet **Mars** were colonized, what effect would it have on . . .

national defense?

scientists?

_____?

Name: _____ **Date:** _____

Eek! A Martian!

www.scholastic.com/profbooks/easyinternet/10fieldtrips.htm

Directions You're studying the Martian surface when, suddenly, two faces appear in your scope! They're Martians—each one completely different from the other, yet both perfectly suited for life on Mars. Click on the links under this Web site to learn about the Martian environment. Then sketch the aliens below. Next to each drawing, jot down some notes about how its features are adapted to its environment.

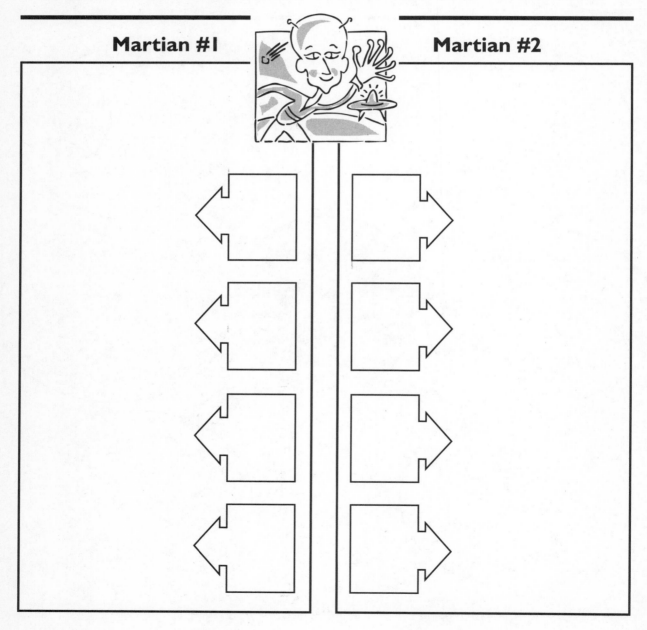

Martian #1

Martian #2

Ellis Island

Gateway to a New Life

Travel Plan

It has been said that the journey of a thousand miles begins with a single step. This is especially true of immigrants who came to the shores of America to forge new lives. Prepare your travelers for a journey to a historic place through which many Americans passed.

Trip Planner

Trip Title: Their Journey, Your Journey
Objective: Travelers will trace the steps and story of an immigrant to America.
Skill: Information management

Trip Title: Entering the Unknown . . .
Objective: Travelers will develop a list of questions from the perspective of an immigrant.
Skills: Productive thinking, synthesis

Trip Title: Dear Friend
Objective: Travelers will tell the story of Ellis Island from the perspective of an employee working at the immigration station.
Skill: Synthesis

Itinerary

Steer students to this online "depot" to start their virtual journey on the Web. Just click on the hot links below the activity title to "transport" students to the Web sites they need to complete the activity.

www.scholastic.com/profbooks/easyinternet/10fieldtrips.htm

Name: _____   **Date:** _____

Their Journey, Your Journey

www.scholastic.com/profbooks/easyinternet/10fieldtrips.htm

Directions Click on the links under this Web site to read an immigrant's tale. Imagine what it would have been like to be in that person's place. Pick four of the most important (or meaningful or interesting) parts of the immigrant's story, then retell them in the spaces below. Explain why you chose each of those pieces to retell.

Part of the Story	Why I Chose This Part

Name: _____   Date: _____

Entering the Unknown...

With More Questions Than Answers!

www.scholastic.com/profbooks/easyinternet/10fieldtrips.htm

Directions Pretend that you're an immigrant preparing to move to a new country. You have a thousand questions, from "Why am I leaving my homeland?" to "Where will I sleep on the ship?" Use the graphic organizer below to come up with as many questions as possible. Then click on the links under this Web site to read some immigrants' stories. Do their stories answer any of your questions?

Before the Journey

During the Voyage

Arriving in America

Dear Friend

www.scholastic.com/profbooks/easyinternet/10fieldtrips.htm

Directions You've just started a new job at the immigration station on Ellis Island. Use the stationery below to write a letter to your best friend about your incredible first day. Describe the immigration station in detail, including your job, the people with whom you work, and the people who come through the station. Include your feelings, not just facts. Then post your letter on the board and read your classmates' letters.

Ancient Greece

Birthplace of Civilization

Travel Plan

Tuck in your toga and step into the past to Ancient Greece! This remarkable civilization is rich with tradition, history, art, literature, exploration, and more. Travelers will parade around the Parthenon, hightail it over to the Temple of Hera, and lay down their heads in their very own Greek slumber chamber.

Trip Planner

Trip Title: My Life as an Ancient Greek
Objective: Travelers will apply historical information to personal experience.
Skill: Information management

Trip Title: Welcome to Our Fair City
Objective: Travelers will participate in a simulation centered around ancient times.
Skills: Synthesis, simulation

Trip Title: A Nation in Ruins
Objective: Travelers will explore the importance of archaeological evidence when learning about a culture.
Skills: Evaluation, synthesis

Itinerary

Steer students to this online "depot" to start their virtual journey on the Web. Just click on the hot links below the activity title to "transport" students to the Web sites they need to complete the activity.

www.scholastic.com/profbooks/easyinternet/10fieldtrips.htm

Name: _____   **Date:** _____

My Life as an Ancient Greek

www.scholastic.com/profbooks/easyinternet/10fieldtrips.htm

 Directions Click on the links under this Web site to read about the lifestyles of the different groups of people from Ancient Greece. Then return to the present and create a log of your activities as an Ancient Greek from sunup to nighttime. The schedule below is divided into two-hour blocks. Record what you did, where, and how.

6:00 – 8:00 A.M.	
8:00 – 10:00 A.M.	
10:00 – 12:00 P.M.	
12:00 – 2:00 P.M.	
2:00 – 4:00 P.M.	
4:00 – 6:00 P.M.	
6:00 – 8:00 P.M.	
8:00 – 10:00 P.M.	

Name: _____   Date: _____

Welcome to Our Fair City

www.scholastic.com/profbooks/easyinternet/10fieldtrips.htm

Directions Relive ancient Greece for a day right in your own classroom. You can build scenery, write scripts, bring food … it's up to you (and your teacher)! To prepare for the big day, click on the links under this Web site. As a class, decide what characters you'll need—senators, soldiers, athletes, store owners, slaves. Then, create your own character with a specific job below. On the day of the simulation, you must stay in character for the entire event.

1 My character's name is _____.

2 My character's job is _____.

3 Costume ideas:

_____

4 Relationships my character has with other characters in the simulation:

_____

_____

5 Things my character will do during the simulation:

_____

_____

_____

6 My character is important to this civilization because

_____

_____

_____

Name: _____ **Date:** _____

A Nation in Ruins

www.scholastic.com/profbooks/easyinternet/10fieldtrips.htm

Directions Click on the links under this Web site to study images of the ruins of Ancient Greece. What do the ruins tell you about that civilization? Its history? Its culture? Choose one significant ruin and draw a picture of it on the back of this page. Then write what you think the ruin tells us about the people who once strolled through its hallways and looked out its windows.

_____

_____

_____

_____

_____

_____

_____

_____

Plymouth Rock

Travel Plan

There's a mystery to be solved on this trip into the past. Just what was Plymouth Rock and did anyone actually land on it? What if the Pilgrims landed in, say, Virginia? How different would our country be today? Grab your cloak and funny hat 'cause it's travel time!

Trip Planner

Trip Title: The Name Is Rock, Plymouth Rock
Objective: Travelers will tell the real story of Plymouth Rock from the rock's perspective.
Skills: Knowledge, comprehension

Trip Title: What If…
Objective: Travelers will hypothesize about the landing of the *Mayflower*—on a different site!
Skills: Synthesis, creativity

Trip Title: From the *Mayflower* to the Declaration of Independence
Objective: Travelers will compare the Mayflower Compact to the Declaration of Independence.
Skill: Evaluation

Itinerary

Steer students to this online "depot" to start their virtual journey on the Web. Just click on the hot links below the activity title to "transport" students to the Web sites they need to complete the activity.

www.scholastic.com/profbooks/easyinternet/10fieldtrips.htm

The Name is Rock, Plymouth Rock

www.scholastic.com/profbooks/easyinternet/10fieldtrips.htm

Directions Your mission is to tell the REAL story of Plymouth Rock. Click on the links under this Web site to construct the true story of this sedentary stone. Your story will be picked up by newspapers all over the country, so be sure to get your facts straight and make them interesting!

Plymouth Rock Has Its Day

_____

_____

_____

_____

_____

_____

_____

_____

_____

What If...

www.scholastic.com/profbooks/easyinternet/10fieldtrips.htm

Directions Say that the Pilgrims didn't land in New England but in Virginia, where they were originally headed. How would the history and development of the United States be different today? Use the space below to rewrite history in paragraph form or create a new time line of events in American history. (Remember that the Pilgrims' landing exists within a time line of other events that came before and after it, and all those events are intertwined into our history!)

If the Pilgrims had landed in Virginia . . .

From the Mayflower to the Declaration of Independence

www.scholastic.com/profbooks/easyinternet/10fieldtrips.htm

Directions Click on the links under this Web site to read the Mayflower Compact and the Declaration of Independence. Compare the two documents. What do they have in common? What is different about them? Complete the Venn diagram below to help you compare these two important works.

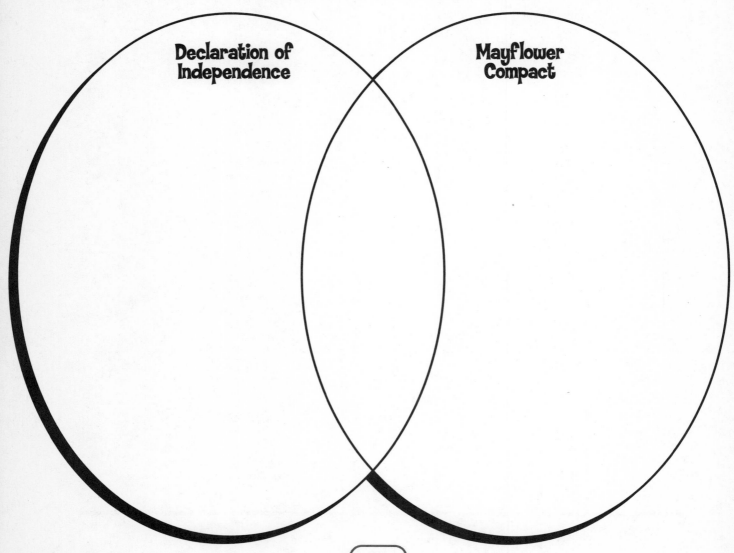

Declaration of Independence

Mayflower Compact

Appendix

Creating Your Own

● PLANNING & PACKING

Decide on your curriculum.

ALWAYS make the learning come first. Make sure your trip has a sound educational purpose, not just an exercise in using the Internet. Know what content exposure or learning experience you want your students to have.

Collect your Web sites.

Plan on having five to 10 final site selections for your trip. But when you first start looking, collect more than you need, then pare them down later. The most important factors in choosing Web sites for students are readability and usability. Can the students read the Web site? Is the Web site easy to use? Let these two factors guide your site selections.

Create your activities.

Creating Web-based activities is the same as creating text-based activities. Just look at the Internet as another source of information. What would you have your students do if they were looking at a picture of a shark? Maybe brainstorm ways the shark is adapted to its environment. You can do the same thing if your students are looking at an online camera of a shark tank.

Internet Field Trips

There are two kinds of Web-based activities: online and off-line. Online activities require the student to be online to do the activity, while off-line activities can be done after the student has had the online experience. For example, most data-collection activities are online (like the one on page 18), while the activity on page 19 can be done almost entirely off-line. Give your students a good mix of tasks to do, too. Whether it's data collection, decision making, or any other kind of task, give them some variety and the trip will be more enjoyable for everyone!

THE JOURNEY
Bon Voyage!

Once you're done with Planning & Packing, the rest is all downhill. Now all you need to do is enjoy the trip!

WELCOME HOME!
How Was Your Trip?

It's very important to take the time to evaluate your trip in two different ways. First, evaluate your trip for and with your students. Did they take from this trip the learning that you wanted them to experience? Did they get from it more than you hoped? Did they learn anything during the trip? Second, evaluate this trip from your perspective as the teacher. Did the sites work? Did the computers work? Did you do a good job organizing the trip? Did the mechanics of groups and numbers of students and machines work? What changes would you make if you did this trip again?

Notes